first phrases
SPANISH

¿Qué trabajo te gustaría tener?

Quiero ser artista.

Illustrated by
Andy Mansfield, Kait Eaton & Sebastian Iwohn

Contents

first phrases
SPANISH

ACKNOWLEDGEMENTS

Publishing Director	Piers Pickard
Publisher	Hanna Otero
Commissioning Editor	Catharine Robertson
Project Management	Duck Egg Blue
Illustrators	Andy Mansfield
	Kait Eaton
	Sebastian Iwohn
Design	Duck Egg Blue
Print Production	Lisa Taylor

With thanks to Rosa Plana, Vega Briega, Tina Garcia and Ernesto Suarez

Published in June 2020 by Lonely Planet Global Ltd
CRN: 554153
ISBN: 978 1 83869 088 5
www.lonelyplanetkids.com
© Lonely Planet 2020
Printed in Singapore

10 9 8 7 6 5 4 3 2 1

Lonely Planet Offices

AUSTRALIA
The Malt Store, Level 3, 551 Swanston St,
Carlton, Victoria 3053
T: 03 8379 8000

IRELAND
Unit E, Digital Court, The Digital Hub,
Rainsford St, Dublin 8

USA
Suite 208, 155 Filbert Street, Oakland, CA 94607
T: 510 250 6400

UK
240 Blackfriars Rd, London SE1 8NW
T: 020 3771 5100

STAY IN TOUCH lonelyplanet.com/contact

How to use this book

Hello! ¡Hola! This book is full of useful Spanish phrases to get you speaking the language. The speech bubble below shows how each phrase is displayed in the book. At the top is the phrase in English. Below that is the phrase in Spanish. And below that is the pronunciation to help you sound out the Spanish words. Try reading the phrases in the book aloud. Practise them with friends, family and whenever you can!

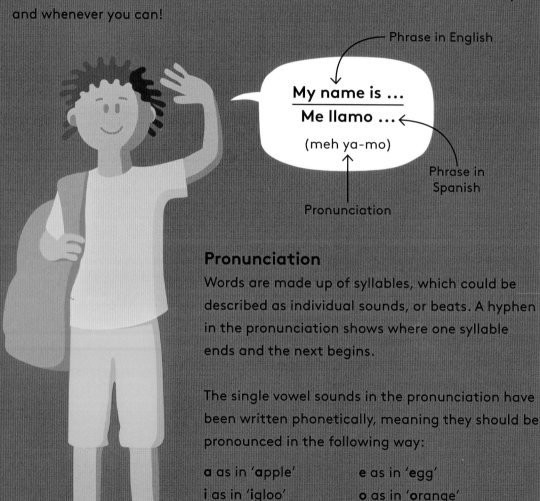

Phrase in English

My name is ...

Me llamo ...

(meh ya-mo)

Phrase in Spanish

Pronunciation

Pronunciation

Words are made up of syllables, which could be described as individual sounds, or beats. A hyphen in the pronunciation shows where one syllable ends and the next begins.

The single vowel sounds in the pronunciation have been written phonetically, meaning they should be pronounced in the following way:

a as in 'apple'   e as in 'egg'
i as in 'igloo'   o as in 'orange'
u as in 'umbrella'

y is pronounced as it sounds in 'yellow'

About the language

The Spanish language has its own set of rules. Here are some guidelines to keep in mind. This book will give you additional helpful notes as you go along, too.

Nouns

A noun is a word that refers to a person, place or thing. Every noun in Spanish is either masculine or feminine. This is its gender, and it affects many of the words around the noun. Some nouns also change depending on their gender.

TIP!
Always try to learn Spanish nouns with el, la, un or una so that you remember their gender.

friend (*male*)	friend (*female*)
amigo	**amiga**
(a-mee-goh)	(a-mee-ga)

El, la, los or las

For '**the**', you say '**el**' (pronounced 'el') or '**la**' (la) depending on the noun's gender. If a noun is masculine, you say **el**. If a noun is feminine, you say **la**.

the boy	the girl
el niño	**la niña**
(el neen-yoh)	(la neen-ya)

If the noun is plural (meaning there is more than one of them), you say '**los**' (los) or '**las**' (las). If the noun is masculine, you say **los**. If the noun is feminine, you say **las**. If the noun includes both masculine and feminine people or objects, you use **los**.

the boys	the girls	the children
los niños	**las niñas**	**los niños**
(los neen-yos)	(las neen-yas)	(los neen-yos)

Un or una

For 'a', you say 'un' (oon) or 'una' (oo-na). If a noun is masculine, you say **un**. If a noun is feminine, you say **una**. For 'some', you say 'unos' (oo-nos) if the noun is masculine and 'unas' (oo-nas) if the noun is feminine.

a dog	a house	some dogs	some houses
un perro	**una casa**	**unos perros**	**unas casas**
(oon peh-rro)	(oo-na ka-sa)	(oo-nos peh-rros)	(oo-nas ka-sas)

Plurals

If a noun ends in a vowel, you add **-s** at the end to make it plural. If a noun ends in a consonant, you add **-es**.

a road	some roads	the hotel	the hotels
una calle	**unas calles**	**el hotel**	**los hoteles**
(oo-na ka-yeh)	(unas ka-yehs)	(el oh-tel)	(los oh-tel-es)

Adjectives

Adjectives are words that describe a noun. In Spanish, they usually end in **-o**, **-a**, **-os** or **-as** depending on whether the noun is masculine, feminine or plural. If the noun is masculine, you leave the adjective ending in **-o**. If the noun is feminine, you change the ending of the adjective to **-a**. If the noun is plural and the adjective ends in a vowel, you add **-s** to the end of the adjective. If the noun is plural and the adjective ends in a consonant, you add **-es**.

In Spanish, the adjective usually comes after the noun.

a small dog	a small house	some red coats
un perro pequeño	**una casa pequeña**	**unos abrigos rojos**
(oon peh-rroh peh-kayn-yo)	(oo-na ka-sa peh-kayn-ya)	(oo-nos a-bree-gos ro-hos)

Pronouns

Pronouns (such as '**he**', '**she**', '**we**', '**yours**') replace a noun or group of nouns. For example, instead of saying 'My mum, my brother and I are going', you could say 'We are going'. The pronoun you use depends on whether the noun it is replacing is masculine (m), feminine (f) or plural. If the noun includes a mix of both masculine and feminine people or objects, you use the masculine version of the pronoun. So in the example above, you say 'Nosotros vamos'.

Pronoun	Translation	Pronunciation
I	**yo**	(yoh)
you (singular, informal)	**tú**	(too)
you (singular, formal)	**usted**	(oo-sted)
he/it (m)	**él**	(el)
she/it (f)	**ella**	(eh-ya)
we	**nosotros (m)/nosotras (f)**	(no-so-tros /no-so-tras)
you (plural, informal)	**vosotros (m)/vosotras (f)**	(bo-so-tros /bo-so-tras)
you (plural, formal)	**ustedes**	(oo-sted-es)
they (m)	**ellos**	(eh-yos)
they (f)	**ellas**	(eh-yas)

NOTE

Use the informal when speaking to friends, close family and people your age or younger. Use the formal when speaking to a grown-up or someone you don't know very well.

In this book we mostly use the informal.

My and your

Words like '**my**' and '**your**' depend on whether the noun they describe is masculine, feminine or plural.

	Singular Noun	Pronunciation	Plural Noun	Pronunciation
my	**mi**	(mee)	**mis**	(mees)
your (singular, informal)	**tu**	(too)	**tus**	(toos)
your (singular, formal)	**su**	(soo)	**sus**	(soos)
his/her/its	**su**	(soo)	**sus**	(soos)
our	**nuestro (m)** or **nuestra (f)**	(nweh-stro) (nweh-stra)	**nuestros (m)** or **nuestras (f)**	(nweh-stros) (nweh-stras)
your (plural, informal)	**vuestro (m)** or **vuestra (f)**	(bweh-stro) (bweh-stra)	**vuestros (m)** or **vuestras (f)**	(bweh-stros) (bweh-stras)
your (plural, formal)	**su**	(soo)	**sus**	(soos)
their	**su**	(soo)	**sus**	(soos)

my bag	**your flower**	**your biscuits**	**their books**
mi bolsa	**tu flor**	**tus galletas**	**sus libros**
(mee bol-sa)	(too flor)	(toos ga-yeh-tas)	(soos lee-bros)

Stressed syllables

In Spanish, each word has a syllable that is always emphasized when you speak the word aloud. This is where the stress is. If a word ends in a consonant other than -**n** or -**s**, you usually stress the last syllable. If a word ends in a vowel, or -**n** or -**s**, you usually stress the second-to-last syllable. If the word does not follow these rules, there is a stress mark over a letter to show you which part of the word to stress, such as in fantástico (fan-**tas**-tee-koh).

eat	red	fantastic
co<u>mer</u>	<u>ro</u>jo	fan<u>tás</u>tico
(ko-**mair**)	(**ro**-hoh)	(fan-**tas**-tee-koh)

In Spanish, all questions begin with an inverted question mark and finish with a normal one.

The same rule applies to a sentence ending with an exclamation mark. Like this! ¡Así!

Are you ready?
¿Listos?

(lees-tos)

In most areas of Spain the letter 'z' is lisped. This sounds like the 'th' in the English word 'thing'. The letter 'c' is also lisped when it comes before 'e' or 'i'. No letters are lisped in Latin America. This book is based on European Spanish, so lisping is included in the pronunciation.

Yes!
¡Sí!

(see)

No!
¡No!

(noh)

Maybe
Quizá

(kee-tha)

Hello / hi
Hola

(o-la)

The letter 'v' in Spanish is pronounced like the letter 'b'.

Welcome
Bienvenida

(beeyen-beh-nee-da)

'**Bienvenida**' is what you say to welcome a female. You say '**bienvenido**' for a male, and '**bienvenidos**' if you are greeting more than one person.

↑
sun
el sol

(el sol)

Good night
Buenas noches

(bweh-nas noch-es)

See you later!
¡Hasta luego!

(as-ta lweh-goh)

↑
moon
la luna

(la loo-na)

Good day
Buenos días

(bweh-nos dee-as)

Good afternoon
Buenas tardes

(bweh-nas tar-des)

See you soon!
¡Hasta pronto!

(as-ta pron-toh)

Goodbye
Adiós

(a-dee-oss)

↑
star
una estrella

(oo-na es-tray-ya)

13

How are you?
¿Cómo está usted?
(ko-moh es-ta oo-sted)

If you are greeting a friend, say '¿Cómo estás?', '¿Qué tal estás?', or simply '¿Qué tal?'

I'm ...
Estoy ...
(es-toy)

very well
muy bien
(mwee beeyen)

OK
bien
(beeyen)

not good
mal
(mal)

Please
Por favor

(por fa-bor)

Thank you
Gracias

(gra-theeyas)

Thank you very much
Muchas gracias

(moo-chas gra-theeyas)

You're welcome
De nada

(deh na-da)

It's nothing
No hay de qué

(noh aye deh keh)

With pleasure
Un placer

(oon pla-thair)

'Disculpe' can also mean 'sorry'.

I'm sorry
Lo siento

(loh seeyen-toh)

Excuse me
Disculpe

(dees-kool-peh)

When speaking to friends or family, you say '**disculpa**'.

15

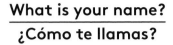

What is your name?
¿Cómo te llamas?

(ko-moh teh ya-mas)

My name is ...
Me llamo...

(meh ya-moh)

Where do you live?
¿Dónde vives?

(don-deh bee-bes)

See pages 154–155 for a list
of country names.

I live ...
Vivo ...

(bee-boh)

in the countryside
en el campo

(en el kam-poh)

in a village
en un pueblo

(en oon pweb-loh)

in a town
en una ciudad

(en oo-na thee-oo-dad)

in a city
en una gran ciudad

(en oo-na gran thee-oo-dad)

I'm pleased to meet you.
Encantado de conocerte.

(eng-kan-ta-doh deh
ko-no-thair-teh)

If you are female,
you would say
'Encantada de conocerte'.

To say how old you are, you say how many years you have.

'Tengo' means 'I have', so if you are ten you say 'Tengo diez años'. This means 'I have ten years'.

How old are you?
¿Cuántos años tienes?
(kwan-tos an-yos teeyeh-nes)

I'm ... years old.
Tengo ... años.
(ten-goh ... an-yos)

1
one
uno
(oo-noh)

2
two
dos
(dos)

7
seven
siete
(seeyeh-teh)

8
eight
ocho
(o-choh)

13
thirteen
trece
(treth-eh)

14
fourteen
catorce
(ka-tor-theh)

15
fifteen
quince
(keen-theh)

16
sixteen
dieciséis
(dee-eh-thee-seh-e

30
thirty
treinta
(trayn-ta)

40
forty
cuarenta
(kwa-ren-ta)

50
fifty
cincuenta
(theeng-kwen-ta)

60
sixty
sesenta
(seh-sen-ta)

3	**4**	**5**	**6**
three	four	five	six
tres	cuatro	cinco	seis
(tres)	(kwat-roh)	(theeng-koh)	(seh-ess)

9	**10**	**11**	**12**
nine	ten	eleven	twelve
nueve	diez	once	doce
(nweh-beh)	(dee-eth)	(on-theh)	(doth-eh)

17	**18**	**19**	**20**
seventeen	eighteen	nineteen	twenty
diecisiete	dieciocho	diecinueve	veinte
-eh-thee-seeyeh-teh)	(dee-eh-theeyo-choh)	(dee-eh-thee-nweb-eh)	(bayn-teh)

70	**80**	**90**	**100**
seventy	eighty	ninety	one hundred
setenta	ochenta	noventa	cien
(seh-ten-ta)	(o-chen-ta)	(no-ben-ta)	(thee-en)

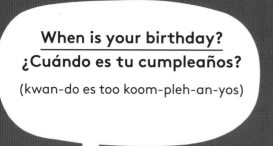

When is your birthday?
¿Cuándo es tu cumpleaños?

(kwan-do es too koom-pleh-an-yos)

My birthday is ...
Mi cumpleaños es ...

(mee koom-pleh-an-yos es)

today
hoy

(oy)

tomorrow
mañana

(man-ya-na)

next week
la semana que viene

(la seh-ma-na keh beeyen-eh)

on Sunday
el domingo

(el do-meeng-oh)

on Monday
el lunes

(el loo-nes)

on Tuesday
el martes

(el mar-tes)

on Wednesday
el miércoles

(el mee-air-ko-les)

on Thursday
el jueves

(el hweb-es)

on Friday
el viernes

(el bee-air-nes)

on Saturday
el sábado

(el sa-ba-doh)

Happy birthday!
¡Feliz cumpleaños!

(feh-leeth koom-pleh-an-yos)

The letter 'ñ' is pronounced like the 'ny' in the English word 'canyon'.

In Spanish days of the week and months don't start with a capital letter.

Here is a present.
Aquí tienes un regalo.

(a-kee teeyeh-nes oon reh-ga-loh)

in January	**in February**	**in March**	**in April**
en enero	**en febrero**	**en marzo**	**en abril**
(en en-eh-roh)	(en feh-breh-roh)	(en mar-thoh)	(en a-breel)

in May	**in June**	**in July**	**in August**
en mayo	**en junio**	**en julio**	**en agosto**
(en ma-yoh)	(en hoon-yoh)	(en hool-yoh)	(en a-gos-toh)

in September	**in October**	**in November**	**in December**
en septiembre	**en octubre**	**en noviembre**	**en diciembre**
(en sep-teeyem-breh)	(en ok-too-breh)	(en no-bee-em-breh)	(en dee-thee-em-breh)

a watch
un reloj

(oon reh-lokh)

yo-yo
un yoyó

(oon yo-yoh)

a toy
un juguete

(oon hoo-get-eh)

a necklace
un collar

(oon ko-yar)

a game
un juego

(oon hweh-go)

What colour is it?
¿De qué color es?
(deh keh ko-lor es)

It is ...
Es ...
(es)

red
rojo
(ro-hoh)

blue
azul
(a-thool)

yellow
amarillo
(a-ma-ree-yoh)

orange
naranja
(na-rang-ha)

purple
morado
(mo-ra-doh)

24

green
verde
(bair-deh)

pink
rosa
(ro-sa)

grey
gris
(grees)

brown
marrón
(ma-rron)

black
negro
(neh-groh)

white
blanco
(blan-koh)

Just like days and months, languages don't begin with a capital letter. Countries do though!

What languages do you speak?
¿Qué idiomas hablas?
(keh ee-deeyo-mas ab-las)

I speak ...
Hablo ...
(ab-loh)

Spanish
español
(es-pan-yol)

English
inglés
(eeng-gles)

Chinese
chino
(chee-noh)

Russian
ruso
(roo-soh)

French
francés
(fran-thes)

German
alemán
(a-leh-man)

I'm sorry. I don't understand.
Lo siento. No entiendo.

(loh seeyen-toh noh en-teeyen-doh)

Could you speak more slowly?
¿Podría hablar más despacio?

(po-dree-a a-blar mas des-pa-theeoh)

What does this say?
¿Qué quiere decir esto?

(keh kee-eh-reh deh-theer es-toh)

sign
el cartel
(el kar-tel)

NO PISAR
EL CÉSPED

It says 'Keep off the grass'.
Dice 'No pisar el césped'.

(dee-theh noh pee-sar el thes-ped)

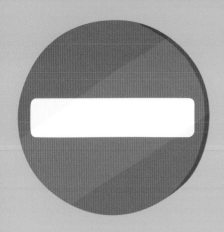

No entry!
¡Prohibido el paso!

(proy-bee-doh el pa-soh)

Warning!
¡Advertencia!

(ad-bair-ten-theeya)

Do not touch!
¡No tocar!

(noh to-kar)

Poison!
¡Veneno!

(beh-neh-noh)

29

Help!
¡Socorro!

(soh-koh-rroh)

It's an emergency!
¡Es una emergencia!

(es oo-na eh-mer-hen-theeya)

Stop!
¡Deténgase!

(deh-ten-ga-seh)

Watch out!
¡Cuidado!

(kwee-da-doh)

I need the police!
¡Necesito a la policía!

(neh-theh-see-toh a la po-lee-thee-a)

There's a fire!
¡Un incendio!

(oon een-then-deeyo)

Please call an ambulance.
Llame a una ambulancia, por favor.

(ya-meh a oo-na am-boo-lan-theeya por fa-bor)

Do you know first aid?
¿Sabe primeros auxilios?

(sa-beh pree-meh-ros owk-see-lyos)

Do you have a mobile phone?
¿Tiene un teléfono móvil?

(teeyen-eh oon teh-leh-fo-noh mo-beel)

Can you help me? I'm lost.
¿Puede ayudarme?
Me he perdido.

(pweh-deh a-yoo-dar-meh meh eh
pair-dee-doh)

Are you OK?
¿Estás bien?
(es-tas beeyen)

I have lost …
He perdido …
(eh pair-dee-doh)

my ticket
mi billete

(mee bee-yeh-teh)

my key
mi llave

(mee ya-beh)

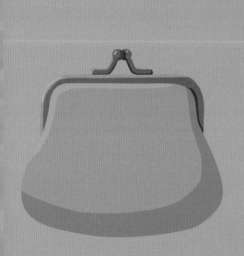

my purse
mi monedero

(mee mo-neh-deh-roh)

my parents
a mis padres

(a mees pa-dres)

Where am I?
¿Dónde estoy?

(don-deh es-toy)

Where is ...
¿Dónde está ...
(don-deh es-ta)

map
un mapa
(oon ma-pa)

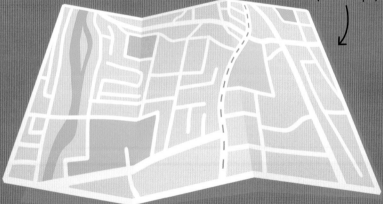

Do you have a map?
¿Tiene un mapa?

(teeyen-eh oon ma-pa)

the hospital?
el hospital?

(el os-pee-tal)

the post office?
la oficina de correos?

(la o-fee-thee-na deh ko-ray-os)

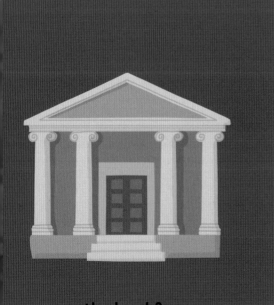

the bank?
el banco?

(el ban-koh)

the nearest toilet?
el aseo más cercano?

(el a-seh-oh mas thair-ka-noh)

It's over there!
¡Está allí!
(es-ta a-yee)

I don't know.
No lo sé.
(noh loh seh)

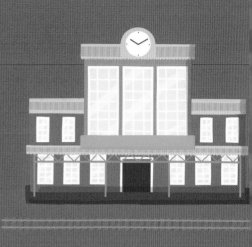

It's next to the train station.
Está junto a la estación de tren
(es-ta hoon-toh a la es-ta-theeyon deh tren)

Is it a long way?
¿Está lejos?
(es-ta leh-hos)

It will take ten minutes.
Se tarda diez minutos.
(seh tar-da dee-eth mee-noo-tos)

It's not far.
No está lejos.
(noh es-ta leh-hos)

Turn right.
Gire a la derecha.

(hee-reh a la deh-reh-tcha)

Turn left.
Gire a la izquierda.

(hee-reh a la eeth-kee-air-da)

Go straight ahead ...
Siga recto ...
(see-ga rek-toh)

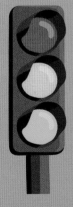

at the traffic lights
en el semáforo

(en el seh-ma-fo-roh)

at the roundabout
en la rotonda

(en la ro-ton-da)

at the crossroads
en el cruce

(en el kroo-theh)

Where are you going?
¿Adónde vais?
(a-don-deh ba-ees)

We are going ...
Vamos ...
(ba-mos)

bus
el autobús
(el ow-toh-boos)

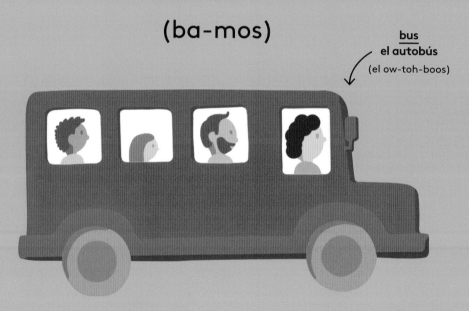

Can I come?
¿Puedo ir?
(pweh-doh eer)

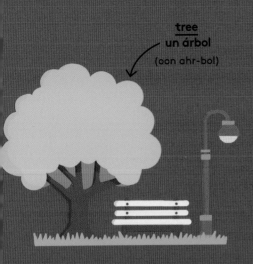

tree
un árbol
(oon ahr-bol)

to the park
al parque

(al par-keh)

to the restaurant
al restaurante

(al rest-ow-ran-teh)

to the swimming pool
a la piscina

(a la pees-thee-na)

to the cinema
al cine

(al thee-neh)

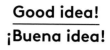

Let's go shopping!
¡Vamos de compras!
(ba-mos deh kom-pras)

Good idea!
¡Buena idea!
(bwen-a ee-deh-a)

at the supermarket
en el supermercado
(en el soo-pair-mair-ka-doh)

at the bakery
en la panadería
(en la pa-na-deh-ree-a)

Where shall we meet?
¿Dónde quedamos?
(don-deh keh-da-mos)

I'll meet you ...
Quedamos ...
(keh-da-mos)

Carnicería

at the butcher
en la carnicería
(en la kar-nee-theh-ree-a)

at the market
en el mercado
(en el mair-ka-doh)

Panadería

It's open.
Está abierto.
(es-ta a-bee-air-toh)

Is it open?
¿Está abierto?
(es-ta a-bee-air-toh)

It's closed.
Está cerrado.

(es-ta theh-rra-doh)

It opens at ten o'clock.
Abierto a las diez.

(a-bee-air-toh a las dee-eth)

It closes at midday.
Cerrado a mediodía.

(theh-rra-doh a meh-deeyo-dee-a)

Let's go somewhere else.
Vamos a otro sitio.

(ba-mos a o-tro see-tee-oh)

43

I would like to buy ...

Quisiera comprar ...

(kee-seeyeh-ra kom-prar)

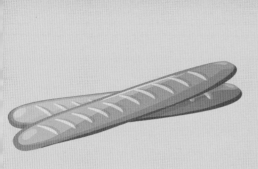

bread
pan

(pan)

milk
leche

(leh-tchay)

butter
mantequilla

(man-teh-kee-ya)

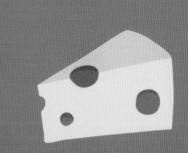

cheese
queso

(keh-soh)

ham
jamón

(ha-mon)

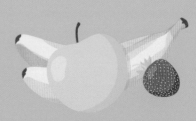

fruit
fruta

(froo-ta)

45

Did you bring ...
¿Has traído ...
(as tra-ee-doh)

the shopping list?
la lista de la compra?

(la lee-sta deh la kom-pra)

a shopping bag?
una bolsa de la compra?

(oo-na bol-sa deh la kom-pra)

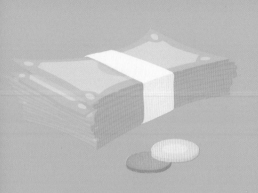

some money?
dinero?

(dee-neh-roh)

a credit card?
una tarjeta de crédito?

(oo-na tar-heh-ta deh kreh-dee-toh)

Here's a basket.
Toma una cesta.

(to-ma oo-na thes-ta)

I'll push the trolley.
Yo empujo el carrito.

(yoh em-poo-hoh el ka-rree-toh)

Do you have ...
¿Tiene ...
(teeyen-eh)

shop assistant (f)
la dependienta
(la deh-pen-dee-en-ta)

till
la caja
(la ka-ha)

toothpaste?
pasta de dientes?

(pa-sta deh deeyen-tes)

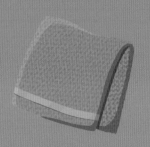

a flannel?
una toalla de cara?

(oo-na to-a-ya deh ka-ra)

shampoo?
champú?

(cham-poo)

toilet paper?
papel higiénico?

(pa-pel ee-hee-eh-nee-koh)

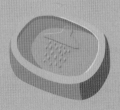

soap?
jabón?

(ha-bon)

a hairbrush?
un cepillo?

(oon seh-pee-yoh)

If the noun you are talking about
is feminine, you would say
'¿Cuántas ... querría?'

pineapples
piñas (f)

(peen-yas)

**How many ...
would you like?**
¿Cuántos ... querría?

(kwan-tos ... keh-ree-a)

apples
manzanas (f)

(man-tha-nas)

sweets
caramelos

(ka-ra-mel-os)

croissants
cruasanes

(krwa-sa-nes)

I would like three please.
Querría tres por favor.

(keh-ree-a tres por fa-bor)

50

That is nice.
Ese está bien.

(eh-seh es-ta beeyen)

There's so much choice.
Hay mucha variedad.

(aye moo-cha ba-ree-ed-ad)

They look good.
Tienen buena pinta.

(teeyen-en bwen-a peen-ta)

It's fantastic!
¡Es fantástico!

(es fan-tas-tee-koh)

This is OK.
Este está bien.

(eh-steh es-ta beeyen)

I like it.
Me gusta.

(meh goo-sta)

How much is …
¿Cuánto cuesta …
(kwan-toh kwes-ta)

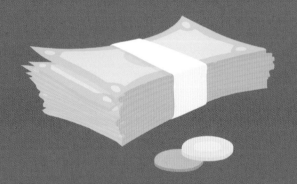

the ball?
la pelota?

(la peh-lo-ta)

the notepad?
el cuaderno?

(el kwa-dair-no)

stamp
el sello

(el say-yoh)

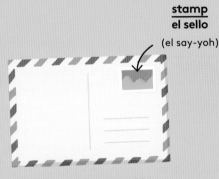

the postcard?
la postal?

(la pos-tal)

the kite?
la cometa?

(la ko-meh-ta)

the bucket?
el cubo?

(el koo-boh)

the spade?
la pala?

(la pa-la)

53

How much are ...
¿Cuánto cuestan ...
(kwan-toh kwes-tan)

the sunglasses?
las gafas de sol?

(las ga-fas deh sol)

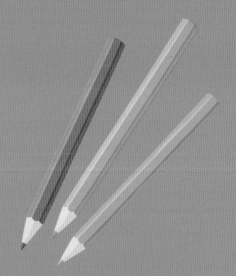

the pencils?
los lápices?

(los la-pee-thes)

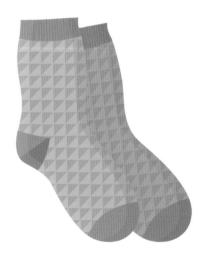

the socks?
los calcetines?

(los kal-theh-tee-nes)

the flowers?
las flores?

(las flor-es)

56

mug
una taza
(oo-na ta-tha)

3€

I don't have enough money.
No tengo suficiente dinero.

(noh ten-goh soo-fee-theeyen-teh
dee-neh-roh)

I'll just have one.
Me quedo solo uno.

(meh keh-doh so-loh oo-noh)

50¢

key ring
el llavero
(el ya-beh-roh)

statue
la estatua
(la es-ta-twa)

450€

It's cheap!
¡Es barato!

(es ba-ra-toh)

It's expensive!
¡Es caro!

(es ka-roh)

57

What's the time?
¿Qué hora es?
(keh o-ra es)

The time is ...
Son las ...
(sohn las)

clock
un reloj
(oon re-lokh)

five o'clock
cinco en punto

(theeng-koh en poon-toh)

quarter past five
cinco y cuarto

(theeng-koh ee kwar-toh)

half past five
cinco y media

(theeng-koh ee meh-deeya)

quarter to six
seis menos cuarto

(seh-ess men-os kwar-toh)

midday
mediodía

(meh-deeyo-dee-a)

midnight
medianoche

(meh-deeya-no-cheh)

59

morning
la mañana
(la man-ya-na)

afternoon
la tarde
(la tar-deh)

In Spanish, afternoon and evening are the same: **'la tarde'**.

evening
la tarde
(la tar-deh)

night
la noche
(la no-cheh)

What time do you get up?
¿A qué hora te levantas?
(a keh o-ra teh leh-ban-tas)

I get up at quarter past six.
Me levanto a las seis y cuarto.
(meh leh-ban-toh a las seh-ess ee kwar-toh)

What time do you go to school?
¿A qué hora vas al colegio?

(a keh o-ra bas al ko-leh-heeyoh)

I go to school at half past eight.
Voy al colegio a las ocho y media.

(boy al ko-leh-heeyoh a las o-choh
ee meh-deeya)

What time do you go to bed?
¿A qué hora te acuestas?

(a keh o-ra teh a-kwes-tas)

That's late!
¡Qué tarde!

(keh tar-deh)

I go to bed at ten o'clock.
Me acuesto a las diez.

(meh a-kwes-toh a las dee-eth)

Let me introduce you to …
Te presento a …

(teh pres-en-toh a)

my mother
mi madre

(mee ma-dreh)

my father
mi padre

(mee pa-dreh)

me
yo
(yoh)

my family
mi familia

(mee fa-mee-leeya)

my sister
mi hermana

(mee air-ma-na)

my brother
mi hermano

(mee air-ma-noh)

Who's this?
¿Quién es este?
(kee-en es eh-steh)

Is this ...
¿Es ...
(es)

Who's that?
¿Quién es ese?
(kee-en es eh-seh)

your aunt?
tu tía?
(too tee-a)

your uncle?
tu tío?
(too tee-oh)

your grandmother?
tu abuela?

(too a-bweh-la)

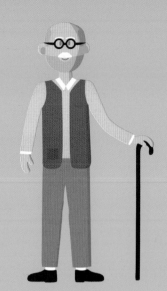

your grandfather?
tu abuelo?

(too a-bweh-loh)

Are they your cousins?
¿Son tus primos?

(sohn toos pree-mos)

Yes.
Sí.

(see)

Do you have any brothers or sisters?
¿Tienes hermanos o hermanas?

(teeyeh-nes air-ma-nos o air-ma-nas)

I have one brother.
Tengo un hermano.

(ten-goh oon air-ma-noh)

**I have two sisters
and three stepbrothers.**
**Tengo dos hermanas y
tres hermanastros.**

(ten-goh dos air-ma-nas ee tres air-ma-nas-tros)

I don't have any siblings.
No tengo hermanos.

(noh ten-goh air-ma-nos)

I am an only child.
Soy hija única (f).

(soy ee-ha oo-nee-ka)

If you are a boy, you say 'Soy hijo único'.

Is your brother older than you?
¿Es tu hermano mayor que tú?

(es too air-ma-noh ma-yor keh too)

He is old.
Él es anciano.

(el es an-theeya-noh)

He is young.
Él es joven.

(el es ho-ben)

My brother is younger than me.
Mi hermano es más joven que yo.
(mee air-ma-noh es mas ho-ben keh yoh)

My brother is older than me.
Mi hermano es mayor que yo.
(mee air-ma-noh es ma-yor keh yoh)

She is old.
Ella es anciana.
(eh-ya es an-theeya-na)

She is very young!
¡Ella es muy joven!
(eh-ya es mwee ho-ben)

What does your sister look like?
¿Cómo es tu hermana?

(ko-moh es tu air-ma-na?)

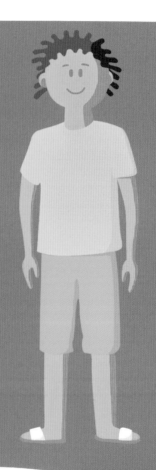

Is she tall or short?
¿Es alta o baja?

(es al-ta oh ba-ha)

71

She has long hair.
Ella tiene el pelo largo.

(eh-ya teeyen-eh el pe-loh lar-goh)

She has short hair.
Ella tiene el pelo corto.

(eh-ya teeyen-eh el pe-loh kor-toh)

She has straight hair.
Ella tiene el pelo liso.

(eh-ya teeyen-eh el pe-loh lee-soh)

She has curly hair.
Ella tiene el pelo rizado.

(eh-ya teeyen-eh el pe-loh ree-tha-doh)

He has ...
Él tiene ...

(el teeyen-eh)

brown hair
el pelo castaño

(el pe-loh kas-tan-yoh)

black hair
el pelo negro

(el pe-loh ne-groh)

red hair
el pelo rojo

(el pe-loh ro-hoh)

blonde hair
el pelo rubio

(el pe-loh roo-byoh)

He has no hair.
No tiene pelo.

(no teeyen-eh pe-loh)

73

She has brown eyes.
Ella tiene los ojos marrones.

(eh-ya teeyen-eh los o-hos ma-rron-es)

She has blue eyes.
Ella tiene los ojos azules.

(eh-ya teeyen-eh los o-hos a-thoo-les

She has grey eyes.
Ella tiene los ojos grises.

(eh-ya teeyen-eh los o-hos gree-ses)

She has green eyes.
Ella tiene los ojos verdes.

(eh-ya teeyen-eh los o-hos bair-des)

He has a beard.
Él tiene barba.

(el teeyen-eh bar-ba)

He has a moustache.
Él tiene bigote.

(el teeyen-eh bee-go-tay)

He has freckles.
Él tiene pecas.

(el teeyen-eh pek-as)

He has a big nose!
¡Él tiene una nariz grande!

(el teeyen-eh oo-na na-reeth gran-day)

What is he wearing?

¿Qué lleva él?

(keh yeh-ba el)

He is wearing ...
Él lleva ...

(el yeh-ba)

a jumper
un jersey

(oon hair-say)

trousers
unos pantalones

(oo-nos pan-ta-lon-es)

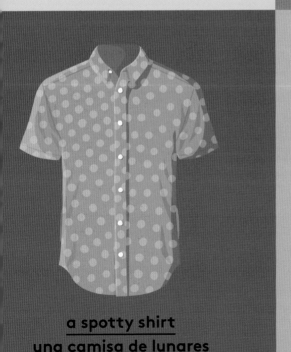

a spotty shirt
una camisa de lunares

(oo-na ka-mee-sa deh loo-na-res)

a striped tie
una corbata de rayas

(oo-na kor-ba-ta deh ra-yas)

What is she wearing?

¿Qué lleva ella?

(keh yeh-ba eh-ya)

She is wearing ...
Ella lleva ...

(eh-ya yeh-ba)

glasses
gafas

(ga-fas)

a cardigan
una chaqueta de punto

(oo-na cha-ket-a deh poon-toh)

a pretty dress
un vestido bonito

(oon bes-tee-doh bon-ee-toh)

grey trainers
zapatillas grises

(tha-pa-tee-yas gree-ses)

'**To be**' can be translated as '**ser**' or '**estar**'. With adjectives, '**estar**' is normally used to describe a temporary situation.

'**Wet**', '**dry**' and '**dirty**' are temporary situations. That's why we use '**estar**' with them.

My T-shirt is ...
Mi camiseta ...
(mee ka-mee-seh-ta)

wet
está mojada

(es-ta mo-ha-da)

dry
está seca

(es-ta seh-ka)

too small
es demasiado pequeña

(es deh-ma-seeyah-doh peh-kayn-ya)

too big
es demasiado grande

(es deh-ma-seeyah-doh gran-day)

dirty
está sucia

(es-ta soo-theeya)

torn
está rasgada

(es-ta ras-ga-da)

81

Do you have any pets?
¿Tienes mascotas?

(teeyeh-nes mas-ko-tas)

I don't have any pets.
No tengo mascotas.

(no ten-goh mas-ko-tas)

Yes, I have two pets.
Sí, tengo dos mascotas.

(see ten-goh dos mas-ko-tas)

I have ...
Tengo ...
(ten-goh)

a mouse
un ratón

(oon ra-ton)

a rabbit
un conejo

(oon ko-neh-hoh)

a cat
un gato

(oon ga-toh)

a horse
un caballo

(oon ka-ba-yoh)

a hamster
un hámster

(oon ham-stair)

a dog
un perro

(oon peh-rroh)

a fish
un pez

(oon peth)

a lizard
un lagarto

(oon la-gar-toh)

a bird
un pájaro

(oon pa-ha-roh)

What's she like?
¿Cómo es ella?

(ko-moh es eh-ya)

He is cute.
Él es guapo.

(el es gwa-poh)

What's he like?
¿Cómo es él?

(ko-moh es el)

She is playful.
Ella es alegre.

(eh-ya es a-leg-reh)

She is funny.
Ella es divertida.

(eh-ya es dee-bair-tee-da)

He is clever.
Él es inteligente.

(el es een-tel-ee-hen-teh)

She is friendly.
Ella es simpática.

(eh-ya es seem-pa-tee-ka)

He is crazy.
Él está loco.

(el es-ta lo-koh)

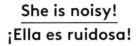

She is noisy!
¡Ella es ruidosa!
(eh-ya es rwee-do-sa)

But I love her.
Pero la quiero.
(peh-roh la kee-eh-roh)

WOOF!
¡GUAU!

Adjectives change depending on whether the thing they are describing is male or female. Remember, adjectives ending in -o usually change to -a if we are talking about a female. Adjectives ending in -e or a **consonant** do not change depending on gender.

Today it's ...
Hoy hace ...
(oy a-theh)

cloud
la nube
(la noo-beh)

hot
calor

(ka-lor)

cold
frío

(free-oh)

fine
buen tiempo

(bwen teeyem-poh)

bad
mal tiempo

(mal teeyem-poh)

What will the weather be tomorrow?
¿Qué tiempo hará mañana?
(keh teeyem-poh a-ra man-ya-na)

Tomorrow it will be ...
Mañana habrá ...
(man-ya-na a-bra)

rainbow
un arco iris
(oon ark-oh ee-rees)

windy
viento

(beeyen-toh)

stormy
tormenta

(tor-men-ta)

cloudy
nubes

(noo-bes)

foggy
niebla

(nee-eh-bla)

It's sunny! I will wear ...

¡Hace sol! Llevaré ...

(a-theh sol yeh-ba-reh)

my cap
mi gorra

(mee go-ra)

some shorts
unos pantalones cortos

(oo-nos pan-ta-lon-es kor-tos)

a T-shirt
una camiseta

(oo-na ka-mee-seh-ta)

It's raining! I need ...
¡Está lloviendo! Necesito ...
(es-ta yo-beeyen-doh
neh-theh-see-toh)

an umbrella
un paraguas

(oon pa-ra-gwas)

a coat
un abrigo

(oon a-bree-goh)

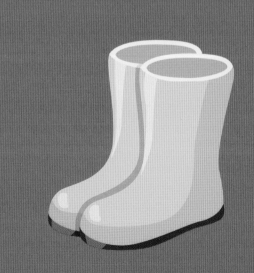

some boots
unas botas

(oo-nas bo-tas)

It's snowing! Where is / are …

¡Está nevando!
¿Dónde está / están …

(es-ta neh-ban-doh
don-deh es-ta/es-tan)

my winter hat?
mi gorro?

(mee go-rroh)

my scarf?
mi bufanda?

(mee boo-fan-da)

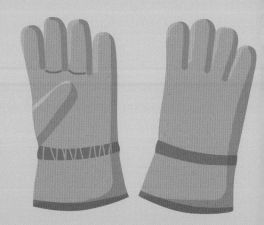

my gloves?
mis guantes?

(mees gwan-tes)

spring
la primavera

(la pree-ma-beh-ra)

summer
el verano

(el beh-ra-no)

The seasons
Las estaciones

(las es-ta-theeyon-es)

autumn
el otoño

(el o-ton-yoh)

winter
el invierno

(el een-bee-air-no)

How do you feel?

¿Cómo te sientes?

(ko-moh teh seeyen-tes)

I feel …

Me siento …

(meh seeyen-toh)

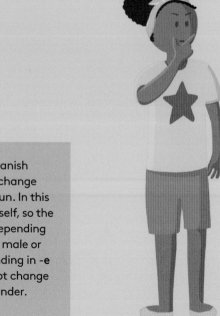

Remember, in Spanish adjectives usually change depending on the noun. In this case, the noun is yourself, so the adjectives change depending on whether you are male or female. Adjectives ending in -**e** or a **consonant** do not change depending on gender.

Are you OK?

¿Estás bien?

(es-tas beeyen)

happy
feliz

(feh-leeth)

sad
triste

(tree-steh)

tired
cansado (m) / cansada (f)

(kan-sa-doh / kan-sa-da)

excited
entusiasmado (m) / entusiasmada (f)

(en-too-seeyas-ma-doh / en-too-seeyas-ma-da)

nervous
nervioso (m) / nerviosa (f)

(nair-bee-os-oh / nair-bee-os-ah)

angry
enfadado (m) / enfadada (f)

(en-fa-da-doh / en-fa-da-da)

I don't feel well!
¡No me encuentro bien!
(noh meh en-kwen-troh beeyen)

I have a cough.
Tengo tos.

(ten-goh tos)

I have a cold.
Tengo catarro.

(ten-goh ka-ta-rroh)

I have a stomach ache.
Me duele el estómago.

(meh dweh-leh el es-to-ma-goh)

I have a headache.
Me duele la cabeza.

(meh dweh-leh la ka-beh-tha)

I have a fever.
Tengo fiebre.

(ten-goh fee-eh-breh)

I feel faint.
Me mareo.

(meh ma-reh-oh)

Where does it hurt?
¿Dónde te duele?
(don-deh teh dwel-eh)

My ... hurts
Me duele ...
(meh dwel-eh)

first aid kit
botiquín
(bo-tee-keen)

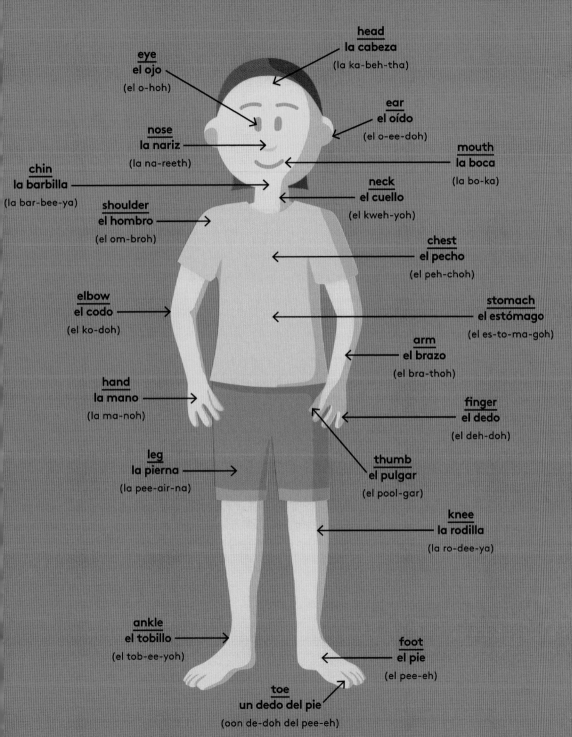

head
la cabeza
(la ka-beh-tha)

eye
el ojo
(el o-hoh)

ear
el oído
(el o-ee-doh)

nose
la nariz
(la na-reeth)

mouth
la boca
(la bo-ka)

chin
la barbilla
(la bar-bee-ya)

neck
el cuello
(el kweh-yoh)

shoulder
el hombro
(el om-broh)

chest
el pecho
(el peh-choh)

elbow
el codo
(el ko-doh)

stomach
el estómago
(el es-to-ma-goh)

arm
el brazo
(el bra-thoh)

hand
la mano
(la ma-noh)

finger
el dedo
(el deh-doh)

leg
la pierna
(la pee-air-na)

thumb
el pulgar
(el pool-gar)

knee
la rodilla
(la ro-dee-ya)

ankle
el tobillo
(el tob-ee-yoh)

foot
el pie
(el pee-eh)

toe
un dedo del pie
(oon de-doh del pee-eh)

99

You need some medicine.
Necesitas una medicina.

(neh-theh-see-tas oo-na meh-dee-thee-na)

medicine
una medicina
(oo-na meh-dee-thee-na)

Go to ...
Ve ...
(beh)

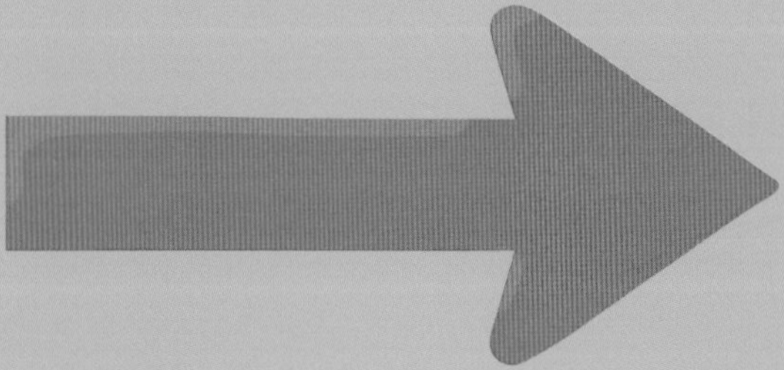

Get well soon!
¡Que te mejores!

(keh teh meh-hor-es)

the pharmacy
a la farmacia

(a la far-ma-theeya)

the doctor's surgery
a la consulta del médico

(a la kon-sool-ta del meh-dee-koh)

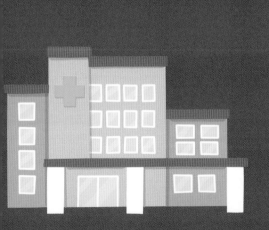

the hospital
al hospital

(al os-pee-tal)

bed
a la cama

(a la ka-ma)

Let's go to the café for ...
Vamos a la cafetería a tomar ...
(ba-mos a la ka-feh-teh-ree-yah a to-mar)

breakfast
el desayuno

(el des-a-yoo-noh)

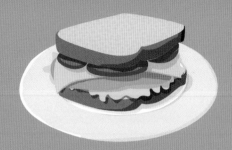

lunch
el almuerzo

(el al-mwair-thoh)

dinner
la cena

(la theh-na)

a drink
una bebida

(oo-na beh-bee-da)

Where shall we sit?
¿Dónde nos sentamos?
(don-deh nos sen-ta-mos)

Let's sit there.
Sentémonos allí.
(sen-teh-mo-nos a-yee)

Do you have Wi-Fi?
¿Tiene Wi-Fi?
(teeyen-eh wee-fee)

Where is the bathroom?
¿Dónde está el baño?
(don-deh es-ta el ban-yoh)

105

Are you ready to order?
¿Desean pedir ya?
(deh-seh-an peh-deer ya)

I would like ...
Quisiera ...
(kee-seeyeh-ra)

an ice cream
un helado

(oon eh-la-doh)

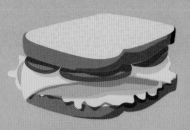

a sandwich
un sándwich

(oon san-weech)

cherry
la cereza
(la theh-reh-tha)

a slice of cake
un trozo de tarta

(oon tro-thoh deh tar-ta)

a salad
una ensalada

(oo-na en-sa-la-da)

a burger
una hamburguesa

(oo-na am-boor-geh-sa)

fries
patatas fritas

(pa-ta-tas free-tas)

And your friend?
¿Y su amigo (m)?
(ee soo a-mee-goh)

He would like ...
Él quisiera ...
(el kee-seeyeh-ra)

water
agua

(a-gwa)

apple juice
un zumo de manzana

(oon thoo-moh deh man-tha-na)

orange juice
un zumo de naranja

(oon thoo-moh deh na-rang-ha)

lemonade
una limonada

(oo-na lee-mo-na-da)

cola
un refresco de cola

(oon reh-fres-koh deh ko-la)

coffee
un café

(oon ka-feh)

What's your favourite flavour?
¿Cuál es tu sabor favorito?
(kwal es too sa-bor fa-bo-ree-toh)

My favourite flavour is ...
Mi sabor favorito es ...
(mee sa-bor fa-bo-ree-toh es)

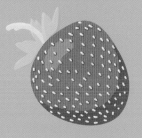

strawberry
fresa
(fray-sa)

vanilla
vainilla
(bay-nee-ya)

hazelnut
avellana

(a-beh-ya-na)

chocolate
chocolate

(tcho-ko-la-teh)

mint
menta

(men-ta)

pistachio
pistacho

(pee-sta-choh)

coconut
coco

(ko-koh)

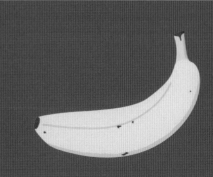

banana
plátano

(pla-ta-noh)

In Spanish, the phrase **'I don't like…'** changes depending on how many things you are talking about.

If you are talking about one thing (singular), you say **'No me gusta…'** and for more than one thing (plural) you say **'No me gustan…'**.

I don't like …
No me gusta / gustan …
(noh meh goo-sta / goo-stan)

Yuk!
¡Puaj!
(pwah)

I don't like chicken either.
A mí tampoco me gusta el pollo.
(a mee tam-po-koh meh goo-sta el po-yoh)

tomatoes
los tomates

(los to-ma-tays)

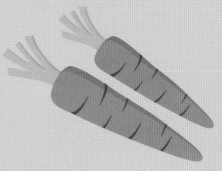

carrots
las zanahorias

(las tha-na-or-ee-as)

chicken
el pollo

(el po-yoh)

noodles
los fideos

(los fee-deh-os)

pasta
la pasta

(la pas-ta)

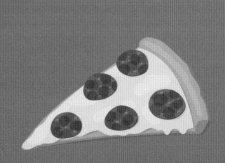

pizza
la pizza

(la peet-tha)

If you are a girl, you would say '**Soy alérgica**'.

I'm allergic to …
Soy alérgico (m) …
(soy a-lair-hee-koh)

nuts
a los frutos secos

(a los froo-tos seh-kos)

milk
a la leche

(a la letch-ay)

fish
al pescado

(al pes-ka-doh)

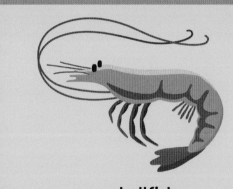

shellfish
al marisco

(al ma-rees-koh)

eggs
a los huevos

(a los way-bos)

wheat
al trigo

(al tree-goh)

Excuse me! I need ...
¡Disculpe! Necesito ...
(dee-skool-peh neh-theh-see-toh)

a plate
un plato
(oon pla-toh)

a bowl
un bol
(oon bol)

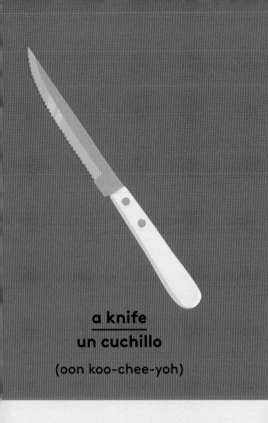

a knife
un cuchillo

(oon koo-chee-yoh)

a fork
un tenedor

(oon teh-neh-dor)

a spoon
una cuchara

(oo-na koo-tcha-ra)

a napkin
una servilleta

(oo-na sair-bee-yeh-ta)

This is delicious!
¡Está buenísimo!

(es-ta bwen-ee-see-moh)

Can I have more ...?
¿Podría tomar más ...?

(po-dree-a to-mar mas)

I don't like this!
¡Esto no me gusta!

(es-toh noh meh goo-sta)

It's horrible!
¡Está malísimo!

(es-ta ma-lee-see-moh)

I can't eat it.
No puedo comerlo.

(noh pweh-doh ko-mair-loh)

Could I order something else?
¿Podría pedir otra cosa?

(po-dree-a peh-deer o-tra ko-sa)

ketchup
el kétchup
(el ketch-oop)

pepper
la pimienta
(la pee-meeyen-ta)

glass
el vaso
(el ba-soh)

salt
la sal
(la sal)

Please can we have the bill?
La cuenta, por favor.

(la kwen-ta por fa-bor)

Where are you going?
¿A dónde vas?
(a don-deh bas)

I'm going to school.
Voy al colegio.
(boy al ko-leh-heeyoh)

Do you like school?
¿Te gusta el colegio?
(teh goo-sta el ko-leh-heeyoh)

Yes, it's good.
Sí, está bien.
(see es-ta beeyen)

I like school.
Me gusta el colegio.
(meh goo-sta el ko-leh-heeyoh)

No, I don't like school!
¡No, no me gusta el colegio!
(noh noh meh goo-sta el ko-leh-heeyoh)

I like school because I see my friends.
Me gusta el colegio porque veo a mis amigos.

(meh goo-sta el ko-leh-heeyoh por-keh bay-oh
a mees a-mee-gos)

girl
la niña

(la neen-ya)

boy
el niño

(el neen-yoh)

My best friend is called ...
Mi mejor amigo se llama ...

(mee meh-hor a-mee-goh seh ya-ma)

If your best friend is female,
you would say '**Mi mejor
amiga se llama...**'

How do you get to school?
¿Cómo vas al colegio?

(ko-moh bas al ko-leh-heeyoh)

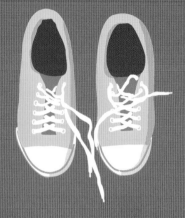

I walk.
Voy andando.

(boy an-dan-doh)

I cycle.
Voy en bicicleta.

(boy en bee-thee-kleh-ta)

I go by scooter.
Voy en patinete.

(boy en pa-tee-neh-teh)

I go in the car.
Voy en coche.

(boy en ko-tchay)

I catch a bus.
Cojo el autobús.

(ko-hoh el ow-toh-boos)

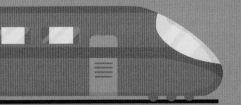

I get the train.
Cojo el tren.

(ko-hoh el tren)

It depends.
Depende.

(de-pen-day)

When it's sunny, I walk.
Si hace sol, voy andando.

(see a-theh sol boy an-dan-doh)

What's your favourite subject?
¿Cuál es tu asignatura favorita?

(kwal es too a-seeg-na-too-ra fa-bo-ree-ta)

My favourite subject is ...
Mi asignatura favorita es ...

(mee a-seeg-na-too-ra
fa-bo-ree-ta es)

It's easy.
Es fácil.

(es fa-theel)

art
dibujo

(dee-boo-hoh)

maths
matemáticas

(ma-tay-ma-tee-kas)

geography
geografía

(heh-o-gra-fee-a)

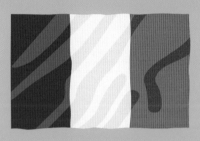

French
francés

(fran-thes)

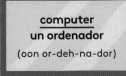

computer
un ordenador

(oon or-deh-na-dor)

computing
informática

(een-for-ma-tee-ka)

music
música

(moo-see-ka)

I don't like ...
No me gusta ...
(noh meh goo-sta)

It's difficult.
Es difícil.

(es dee-fee-theel)

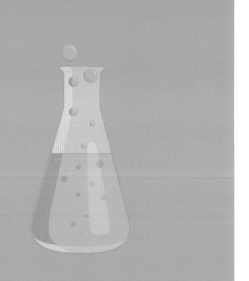

science
ciencias

(thee-en-theeyas)

history
historia

(ee-sto-ree-a)

PE
gimnasia

(heem-na-seeyah)

cookery
cocina

(ko-thee-na)

127

My teacher is great.
Mi profesor es genial.

(mee pro-fess-or es heh-nee-al)

My teacher is helpful.
Mi profesor es muy atento.

(mee pro-fess-or es mwee a-ten-toh)

My teacher is strict!
¡Mi profesor es estricto!

(mee pro-fess-or es es-treek-toh)

He's nice.
Él es amable.

(el es a-ma-bleh)

She's friendly.
Ella es simpática.

(eh-ya es seem-pa-tee-ka)

What is your teacher called?
¿Cómo se llama tu profesor?
(ko-moh seh ya-ma too pro-fess-or)

My teacher is called ...
Mi profesor se llama ...
(mee pro-fess-or seh ya-ma)

Can we sit together?
¿Nos sentamos juntos?
(nos sen-ta-mos hoon-tos)

Let's be friends!
¡Seamos amigos!
(seh-a-mos a-mee-gos)

Do you need help with your work?
¿Necesitas ayuda con las tareas?
(neh-theh-see-tas a-yoo-da kon las ta-reh-as)

What's in your bag?
¿Qué llevas en la mochila?

(keh yeh-bas en la mo-chee-la)

I have ...
Llevo ...

(yeh-boh)

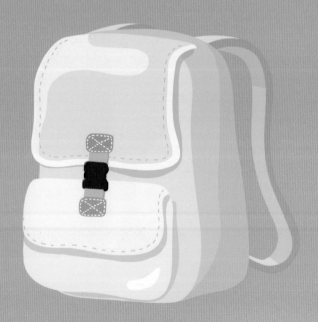

What's that?
¿Qué es eso?

(keh es eh-soh)

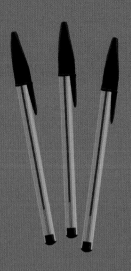

some pens
unos bolis

(oo-nos bo-lees)

my lunch
el almuerzo

(el al-mwer-soh)

a bottle of water
una botella de agua

(oo-na bo-tay-ya deh a-gwa)

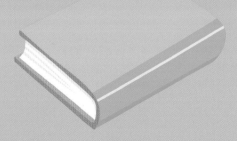

a book
un libro

(oon lee-broh)

131

The pencil is ...
El lápiz está ...
(el la-peeth es-ta)

on the table
sobre la mesa

(soh-breh la meh-sa)

under the chair
debajo de la silla

(deh-ba-hoh deh la see-ya)

inside the pencil case
dentro del estuche

(den-troh del es-too-cheh)

next to the scissors
junto a las tijeras

(hoon-toh a las tee-heh-ras)

in front of the telephone
delante del teléfono

(deh-lan-tay del teh-leh-fo-noh)

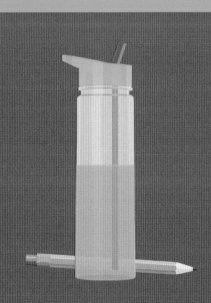

behind the bottle
detrás de la botella

(deh-tras deh la bo-tay-ya)

My hobby is ...
Mi pasatiempo es ...

(mee pa-sa-teeyem-poh es)

My hobbies are ...
Mis pasatiempos son ...

(mees pa-sa-teeyem-pos sohn)

painting
la pintura

(la peen-too-ra)

playing the guitar
tocar la guitarra

(to-kar la gee-ta-rra)

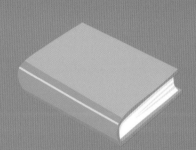

reading
leer

(leh-air)

watching films
ver películas

(bair pel-ee-koo-las)

playing video games
jugar videojuegos

(hoo-gar bee-day-oh-hweh-gos)

dancing
bailar

(bay-lar)

135

What is your favourite sport?
¿Cuál es tu deporte favorito?
(kwal es too deh-por-tay
fa-bo-ree-toh)

My favourite sport is ...
Mi deporte favorito es ...
(mee deh-por-tay fa-bo-ree-toh es)

rugby
el rugby

(el roog-bee)

basketball
el baloncesto

(el ba-lon-thes-toh)

football
el fútbol

(el foot-bol)

swimming
la natación

(la na-ta-thee-on)

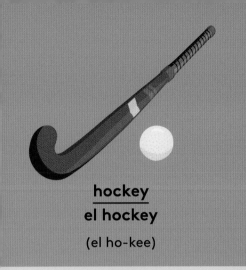

hockey
el hockey

(el ho-kee)

skiing
el esquí

(el es-kee)

horse riding
la equitación

(la ek-ee-ta-thee-on)

volleyball
el voleibol

(el bo-lay-bol)

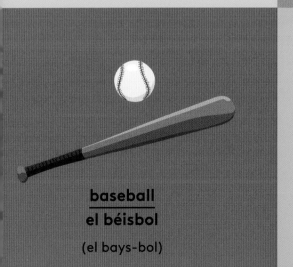

baseball
el béisbol

(el bays-bol)

cricket
el críquet

(el kree-ket)

138

I went to a party
fui a una fiesta

(fwee a oo-na feeyes-ta)

boat
un barco
(oon bar-koh)

I went sailing
fui a navegar

(fwee a na-beh-gar)

I went bowling
jugué a los bolos

(hoo-geh a los bo-los)

I didn't do my homework!
¡No hice los deberes!

(noh ee-theh los deh-bair-res)

I did my homework
hice los deberes

(ee-theh los deh-bair-res)

What are you doing next weekend?

¿Qué harás este fin de semana?

(keh a-ras eh-steh feen deh seh-ma-na)

Next weekend I'm ...
Este fin de semana ...

(eh-steh feen deh seh-ma-na)

How about you?

¿Y tú?

(ee too)

going to the beach
iré a la playa

(ee-reh a la pla-ya)

going cycling
iré en bici

(ee-reh en bee-thee)

going ice skating
iré a patinar sobre hielo

(ee-reh a pa-tee-nar so-bray yeh-loh)

going to play tennis
jugaré al tenis

(hoo-ga-reh al teh-nees)

Let's bake a cake.
Vamos a hacer un pastel.
(ba-mos a a-thair oon pas-tel)

We will need …
Necesitaremos …
(neh-theh-see-ta-rem-os)

We need ingredients, too!
¡También necesitamos ingredientes!
(tam-beeyen neh-theh-see-ta-mos
een-greh-deeyen-tes)

an apron
un delantal

(oon deh-lan-tal)

scales
una balanza

(oo-na ba-lan-tha)

a recipe
una receta

(oo-na reh-theh-tah)

a whisk
unas varillas

(oo-nas ba-ree-yas)

an oven
un horno

(oon or-noh)

I'll help you wash up.
Te ayudo a fregar los platos.

(teh a-yoo-doh a fray-gar los pla-tos)

Yesterday I went to the zoo.
Ayer fui al zoo.
(a-yair fwee al thoor)

I saw ...
Vi ...
(bee)

a lion
un león

(oon lay-on)

a tiger
un tigre

(oon tee-greh)

a giraffe
una jirafa

(oo-na hee-ra-fa)

a zebra
una cebra

(oo-na theh-bra)

a panda
un oso panda

(oon o-soh pan-da)

I had a great time!
¡Me lo pasé muy bien!

(meh loh pa-seh mwee beeyen)

145

My favourite animal is ...
Mi animal favorito es ...
(mee a-nee-mal fa-bo-ree-toh es)

an elephant
el elefante

(el el-ay-fan-tay)

a penguin
el pingüino

(el peeng-gwee-noh)

an owl
el búho

(el boo-oh)

a polar bear
el oso polar

(el o-soh po-lar)

a spider
la araña

(la a-ran-ya)

a monkey
el mono

(el mo-no)

a cow
la vaca

(la ba-ka)

a pig
el cerdo

(el thair-doh)

a meerkat
la suricata

(la soo-ree-ka-ta)

a hedgehog
el erizo

(el eh-ree-tho)

Why?
¿Por qué?
(por keh)

I like koalas because they are cute.
Me gustan los koalas porque son adorables.
(meh goo-stan los ko-a-las por-keh sohn a-do-ra-bles)

I like parrots because they are colourful.
Me gustan los loros porque son de coloridos.
(meh goo-stan los lo-ros por-keh sohn deh ko-lo-ree-dohs)

I like dolphins because they are clever.
Me gustan los delfines porque son inteligentes.

(meh goo-stan los del-fee-nes por-keh sohn een-teh-lee-hen-tes)

I like sharks because they are scary!
¡Me gustan los tiburones porque dan miedo!

(meh goo-stan los tee-boo-ro-nes por-keh dan mee-eh-doh)

149

In Spanish, there is no need to say 'a' when talking about professions.

I want to be ...
Quiero ser ...
(kee-eh-roh sair)

What do you want to be when you grow up?
¿Qué quieres cuando crezcas?
(keh kee-eh-res kwan-doh kres-kas)

a singer
cantante
(kan-tan-tay)

a firefighter
bombero (m) / bombera (f)
(bom-bair-oh / bom-bair-a)

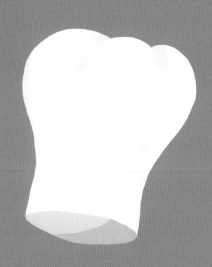

a chef
cocinero (m) / cocinera (f)

(ko-thee-nair-oh / ko-thee-nair-a)

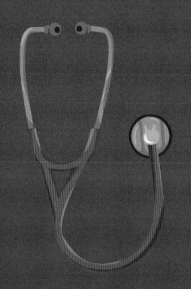

a doctor
médico (m) / médica (f)

(meh-dee-ko / meh-dee-ka)

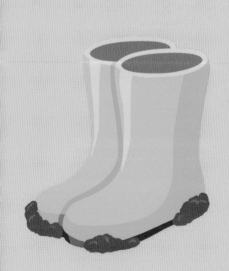

a farmer
granjero (m) / granjera (f)

(gran-hair-oh / gran-hair-a)

a teacher
profesor (m) / profesora (f)

(pro-fess-or / pro-fess-or-a)

What job would you like?
¿Qué trabajo te gustaría tener?
(keh tra-ba-hoh teh
goo-sta-ree-a teh-ner)

I'm not sure yet.
Aún no estoy
seguro (m) / segura (f).
(a-oon noh es-toy
seh-goo-roh / seh-goo-ra)

Would you like to be ...
¿Te gustaría ser ...
(teh goo-sta-ree-a sair)

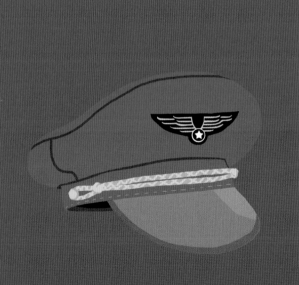

a pilot?
piloto?
(pee-lo-toh)

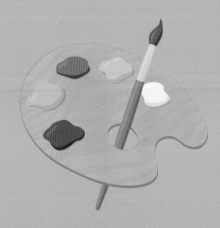

an artist?
artista?
(ar-tee-sta)

a police officer?
policía?

(po-lee-thee-a)

a vet?
veterinario (m) / veterinaria (f)?

(bet-air-ree-na-reeyoh / bet-air-ree-na-reeya)

a plumber?
fontanero (m) / fontanera (f)?

(fon-ta-nair-roh / fon-ta-nair-ra)

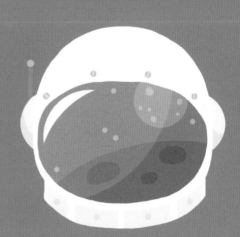

an astronaut?
astronauta?

(a-stro-now-ta)

Are you going on holiday?
¿Te vas de vacaciones?

(teh bas deh ba-ka-theeyoh-nes)

I'm not going on holiday.
No me voy de vacaciones.

(no meh boy deh ba-ka-theeyoh-nes)

I'm staying at home.
Me quedo en casa.

(meh keh-doh en ka-sa)

Yes, I'm going …
Sí, me voy …

(see meh boy)

to Mexico
a México

(a meh-hee-koh)

to the Netherlands
a los Países Bajos

(a los pa-ee-ses ba-hos)

to Canada
a Canadá

(a ka-na-da)

to China
a China

(a chee-na)

to Germany
a Alemania

(a a-leh-ma-neeyah)

to Turkey
a Turquía

(a toor-kee-ah)

to Spain
a España
(a es-pan-ya)

to the United States
a Estados Unidos
(a es-ta-dos oo-nee-dos)

to Australia
a Australia
(a ow-stra-leeya)

to Greece
a Grecia
(a greh-theeya)

to France
a Francia
(a fran-theeya)

**to the
United Kingdom**
al Reino Unido
(al ray-noh oo-nee-doh)

to Thailand
a Tailandia
(a tah-ee-lan-deeya)

to Italy
a Italia
(a ee-ta-leeya)

to South Africa
a Sudáfrica
(a soo-da-free-ka)

to Japan
a Japón
(a ha-pon)

to New Zealand
a Nueva Zelanda
(a nweh-ba theh-lan-da)

to Switzerland
a Suiza
(a swee-tha)

Where are you staying?
¿Dónde te alojas?
(don-deh teh a-lo-has)

I'm staying in ...
Me alojo en ...
(meh a-lo-hoh en)

a hotel
un hotel

(oon oh-tel)

a house
una casa

(oo-na ka-sa)

I'm staying with my family.
Me alojo con mi familia.
(meh a-lo-ho kon mee fa-mee-leeya)

photograph
una foto
(oo-na fo-toh)

a tent
una tienda de campaña
(oo-na teeyen-da deh kam-pan-ya)

a caravan
una caravana
(oo-na ka-ra-ba-na)

How are you getting there?
¿Cómo vas a llegar?

(ko-moh bas a yeh-gar)

I'm going by ...
Voy a ir en ...

(boy a eer en)

Travelling is fun!
¡Viajar es divertido!

(bee-a-har es dee-bair-tee-doh)

car
coche

(ko-tchay)

bus
autobús

(ow-toh-boos)

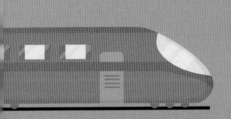

train
tren

(tren)

ferry
ferri

(feh-rree)

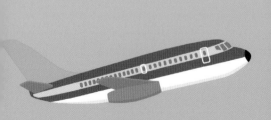

aeroplane
avión

(a-bee-on)

taxi
taxi

(tak-see)

159

What are you taking?
¿Qué te vas a llevar?
(keh teh bas a yeh-bar)

I'm taking ...
Me voy a llevar ...
(meh boy a yeh-bar)

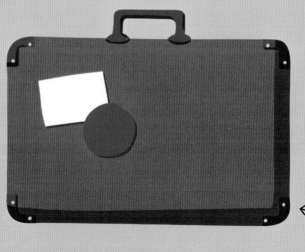

suitcase
una maleta
(oo-na ma-leh-ta)

some sun cream
crema solar

(kray-ma so-lar)

a swimsuit
un bañador

(oon ban-ya-dor)

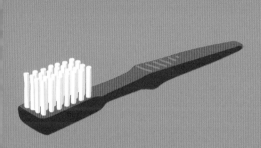

my toothbrush
mi cepillo de dientes

(mee theh-pee-yoh deh deeyen-tes)

a towel
una toalla

(oo-na to-a-ya)

my teddy bear
mi osito de peluche

(mee o-see-toh deh peh-loo-chay)

my passport
mi pasaporte

(mee pa-sa-por-teh)

How long are you staying?
¿Cuánto tiempo te quedas?
(kwan-toh teeyem-poh teh keh-das)

One week.
Una semana.
(oo-na seh-ma-na)

Two weeks.
Dos semanas.
(dos seh-ma-nas)

Just a few days.
Solo unos días.
(so-loh oo-nos dee-as)

It will be amazing!
¡Será increíble!

(seh-ra eeng-kreh-ee-bleh)

It sounds lovely.
Suena muy bien.

(sweh-na mwee beeyen)

Have a good trip!
¡Buen viaje!

(bwen beeya-heh)

See you in a little while.
Hasta pronto.

(as-ta pron-toh)

Enjoy!
¡Pásalo bien!

(pa-sa-loh beeyen)

Goodbye.
Adiós.

(a-dee-oss)

Vocabulary list

Here is a list of English words, along with their Spanish translations. All of these words can be found within the phrases featured in this book.

Some nouns and adjectives change in the feminine form. To make these words feminine add an -a to the end, removing the final -o, if there is one. If the feminine word is very different, the full spelling is given.

a /an	un/una	book (*noun*)	un libro
aeroplane	un avión	boot	una bota
afternoon	la tarde	bottle	una botella
ambulance	una ambulancia	bowl (*noun*)	un bol
and	y	bowling (*noun*)	los bolos
angry	enfadado(a)	boy	un niño
animal	un animal	bread	el pan
apple	una manzana	breakfast	el desayuno
apron	un delantal	brother	un hermano
art	el dibujo	brown	marrón
artist	un(a) artista	bucket	un cubo
astronaut	un(a) astronauta	burger	una hamburgesa
aunt	una tía	bus	un autobús
autumn	el otoño	but	pero
		butchers (*shop*)	una carnicería
bad	malo(a)	butter	la mantequilla
bag	una bolsa/una mochila		
bakery	una panadería	café	una cafetería
ball	una pelota	cake	un pastel
balloon	un globo	cap (*hat*)	una gorra
banana	un plátano	car	un coche
bank	un banco	caravan	una caravana
baseball	el béisbol	card	una tarjeta
basket	una cesta	cardigan	una chaqueta de punto
basketball	el baloncesto	carrot	una zanahoria
bathroom	el baño	cat	un gato
beach	una playa	chair	una silla
beard	una barba	cheese	el queso
because	porque	chef	un(a) cocinero(a)
bed	una cama	chicken	el pollo
behind	detrás	chocolate	el chocolate
bike	una bicicleta	choice	una variedad
bill (*noun*)	la cuenta	cinema	un cine
bird	un pájaro	city	una gran ciudad
birthday	un cumpleaños	clever	inteligente
black	negro(a)	clock	un reloj
blonde	rubio(a)	closed (*adj*)	cerrado(a)
blue	azul	cloud	una nube
boat	un barco	coat	un abrigo

coconut	un coco	fever	la fiebre
coffee	un café	film (noun)	una película
cola	un refresco de cola	fine (adj)	bien
cold (adj)	frío(a)	fire (noun)	un incendio
cold (noun)	un resfriado	firefighter	un(a) bombero(a)
colour	un color	first aid	los primeros auxilios
computer	un ordenador	fish (noun)	un pez
computing	la informática	flannel	una toalla de cara
cookery	la cocina	flower	una flor
cough (noun)	una tos	fog	la niebla
countryside	el campo	football	el fútbol
cousin	un(a) primo(a)	fork	un tenedor
cow	una vaca	freckles	las pecas
crazy	loco(a)	friend	un(a) amigo(a)
credit card	una tarjeta de crédito	friendly	simpático(a)
cricket (sport)	el críquet	fries	unas patatas fritas
crossroads	un cruce	fruit	la fruta
curly	rizado(a)	fun	divertido(a)
cute	guapo(a)	funny	divertido(a)
delicious	buenísimo(a)	game	un juego
difficult	difícil	geography	la geografía
dinner	la cena	giraffe	una jirafa
dirty	sucio(a)	girl	una niña
doctor	un médico	glass (vessel)	un vaso
dog	un perro	glasses	unas gafas
dolphin	un delfín	glove	un guante
dress (noun)	un vestido	good	bueno(a)
drink (noun)	una bebida	goodbye	adiós
dry	seco(a)	grandfather	un abuelo
		grandmother	una abuela
easy	fácil	green	verde
egg	un huevo	grey	gris
elephant	un elefante	guitar	una guitarra
emergency	una emergencia		
evening	la tarde	hair	el pelo
excited	entusiasmado(a)	hairbrush	un cepillo
expensive	caro(a)	ham	el jamón
eye	un ojo	hamster	un hámster
		happy	feliz
family	una familia	hat (winter)	un gorro
fantastic	fantástico(a)	hazelnut	una avellana
farmer	un(a) granjero(a)	hedgehog	un erizo
father	un padre	hello	hola
favourite	favorito(a)	helpful	atento
ferry	un ferri	hi	hola

history	la historia	meerkat	una suricata
hobby	un pasatiempo	menu	la carta
hockey	el hockey	midday	el mediodía
holidays	las vacaciones	midnight	la medianoche
home	una casa	milk	la leche
homework	los deberes	mint	la menta
horse	un caballo	minute	un minuto
horse riding	la equitación	mobile phone	un teléfono móvil
hospital	un hospital	money	el dinero
hot	el calor	monkey	un mono
hotel	un hotel	moon	la luna
house	una casa	more	más
how	cómo	more than	más que
hungry	hambriento(a)	morning	la mañana
		mother	una madre
I	yo	mouse	un ratón
ice cream	un helado	moustache	un bigote
ice skating (noun)	el patinaje sobre hielo	mug	una taza
idea	una idea	music	la música
in front of	delante de		
ingredient	un ingrediente	name	un nombre
		napkin	una servilleta
juice	un zumo	necklace	un collar
jumper	un jersey	nervous	nervioso(a)
		night	la noche
ketchup	el kétchup	no	no
key	una llave	noisy	ruidoso(a)
key ring	un llavero	noodles	los fideos
kite	una cometa	notepad	un cuaderno
knife	un cuchillo	nothing	nada
koala	un koala	nut	un fruto seco
language	un idioma	old	anciano(a)
left (not right)	izquierda	on	en/sobre
lemonade	una limonada	open (adj)	abierto(a)
lion	un león	or	o
lizard	un lagarto	orange (adj)	naranja
long	largo(a)	orange (fruit)	una naranja
lunch	el almuerzo	oven	un horno
		over there	allí
map	un mapa	owl	un búho
market	un mercado		
maths	las matemáticas	panda	un oso panda
maybe	quizá	parent	un padre
me	yo	park (noun)	un parque
medicine	una medicina	parrot	un loro

party (*noun*)	una fiesta	salt	la sal
passport	un pasaporte	sandwich	un sándwich
pasta	la pasta	scarf	una bufanda
PE	la gimnasia	scary	que da miedo
pen	un boli	school	el colegio
pencil	un lápiz	science	las ciencias
pencil case	un estuche	scissors	las tijeras
penguin	un pingüino	season (*time*)	la estación
pepper (*spice*)	la pimienta	shampoo	el champú
pharmacy	una farmacia	shark	un tiburón
phone	un teléfono	shellfish	el marisco
photograph	una fotografía / una foto	shirt	una camisa
pig	un cerdo	shoe	un zapato
pilot	un(a) piloto	shop assistant	un(a) dependiente(a)
pineapple	una piña	shopping list	una lista de la compra
pink	rosa	short	bajo(a) / corto(a)
pistachio	el pistacho	shorts	un pantalón corto
pizza	una pizza	since	desde
plate	un plato	singer	un(a) cantante
playful	alegre	sister	una hermana
please	por favor	skiing (*noun*)	el esquí
plumber	un(a) fontanero(a)	slice (*noun*)	un trozo / una porción
poison	el veneno	small	pequeño(a)
polar bear	un oso polar	soap	el jabón
police	la policía	sock	un calcetín
police officer	un(a) policía	some	algunos (algunas)
postcard	una postal	spade	una pala
post office	una oficina de correos	spider	una araña
present	un regalo	spoon	una cuchara
purple	morado(a)	sport	un deporte
purse	un monedero	spots	unos lunares
		spring (*season*)	la primavera
rabbit	un conejo	stamp (*noun*)	un sello
rain	la lluvia	star	una estrella
rainbow	un arco iris	statue	una estatua
ready	preparado(a)	storm (*noun*)	una tormenta
recipe	una receta	straight	recto(a)
red	rojo(a)	straight (*hair*)	liso(a)
restaurant	un restaurante	strawberry	una fresa
right (*not left*)	derecha	strict	estricto(a)
roundabout	una rotonda	stripes	las rayas
rugby	el rugby	subject (*school*)	la asignatura
		suitcase	una maleta
sad	triste	summer	el verano
sailing (*trip*)	navegación	sun	el sol
salad	una ensalada	sun cream	la crema solar

sunglasses	unas gafas de sol	umbrella	un paraguas
supermarket	un supermercado	uncle	un tío
sweet (noun)	un caramelo	under	debajo
swimming (noun)	la natación		
swimming pool	una piscina	vanilla	la vainilla
swimsuit	un bañador	very	muy
		vet	un(a) veterinario(a)
table	una mesa	video game	un videojuego
tall	alto(a)	village	un pueblo
taxi	un taxi	volleyball	el voleibol
teacher	un(a) profesor(a)		
teddy bear	un osito de peluche	watch (noun)	un reloj
tennis	el tenis	water (noun)	el agua
tent	una tienda de campaña	we	nosotros
thank you	gracias	weather	el tiempo
the	el/la	week	una semana
their	su/de ellos	weekend	un fin de semana
they	ellos (ellas)	weighing scales	una balanza
thirsty	sediento(a)	welcome	bienvenido(a)
ticket	un billete	well (adj)	bien
tie (noun)	una corbata	wet	mojado(a)
tiger	un tigre	wheat	el trigo
till (cash register)	una caja	when	cuándo
time (noun)	la hora	where	dónde
tired	cansado(a)	whisk (noun)	unas varillas
today	hoy	white	blanco(a)
together	juntos (juntas)	who	quién
toilet	el aseo	why	por qué
toilet paper	el papel higiénico	Wi-Fi	el wifi
tomato	un tomate	wind (weather)	el viento
tomorrow	mañana	winter	el invierno
toothbrush	un cepillo de dientes	with	con
toothpaste	la pasta de dientes	without	sin
torn	rasgado(a)		
towel	una toalla	yellow	amarillo(a)
town	una ciudad	yes	sí
toy (noun)	un juguete	yesterday	ayer
traffic lights	el semáforo	young	joven
train (noun)	un tren	yo-yo	un yoyó
train station	una estación de tren		
tree	un árbol	zebra	una cebra
trip (noun)	un viaje	zoo	un zoo
trolley	un carrito		
trousers	unos pantalones		
T-shirt	una camiseta		